# Tertullian
Ad Martyras and The Passion of The Holy Martyrs
Perpetua and Felicitas

Tertullian
# Ad Martyras and The Passion of the Holy Martyrs Perpetua and Felicitas

# Tertullian
# Ad Martyras and The Passion of the Holy Martyrs Perpetua and Felicitas

© Lighthouse Publishing 2018

All rights reserved. Without limiting the rights under copyright reserved above, no part of this publication may be reproduced, stored in a retrieval system, or transmitted, in any form or by any means (electronic, mechanical, photocopying, recording or otherwise), without the prior written permission of the copyright owner of this book.

Published by
Lighthouse Christian Publishing
SAN 257-4330
5531 Dufferin Drive
Savage, Minnesota, 55378
United States of America

www.lighthousechristianpublishing.com

# Tertullian

## Introductory Note.

The Second Class of Tertullian's works, according to the logical method I have endeavored to carry out, is that which includes his treatises against the heresies of his times. In these, the genius of our author is brilliantly illustrated, while, in melancholy fact, he is demonstrating the folly of his own final lapse and the wickedness of that schism and heresy into which he fell away from Truth. Were it not that history abounds in like examples of the frailty of the human intellect and of the insufficiency of "man that walketh to direct his steps," we should be forced to a theory of mental decay to account for inconsistencies so gross and for delusions so besotted. "Genius to madness is *indeed* allied," and who knows but something like that imbecility which closed the career of Swift may have been the fate of this splendid wit and versatile man of parts? Charity, admiration and love force this inquiry upon my own mind continually, as I explore his fascinating pages. And the order in which the student will find them in this series, will lead, I think, to similar reflections on the part of many readers. We observe a natural bent and turn of mind, even in his Catholic writings, which indicate his perils. These are more and more apparent in his recent works, as his enthusiasm heats itself into a frenzy which at last becomes a rage. He breaks down by degrees, as in orthodoxy so also in force and in character. It is almost like the collapse of Solomon or of Bacon. And though our own times have produced no example of stars of equal magnitude, to become falling-stars, we have seen illustrations the most humiliating, of those calm words of Bishop Kaye: "Human nature often presents the curious phenomenon of a union of the most opposite qualities in the same mind; of vigor, acuteness and discrimination on some subjects, with imbecility, dullness and bigotry on others." Milton, himself another example of his own threnode, breaks forth in this splendid utterance of lyrical confession:

> "God of our fathers what is man?
>     Nor do I name of men the common rout,
>     That, wandering loose about,
> Grow up and perish as the summer fly,
> Heads without name, no more remembered,
> But such as thou hast solemnly elected,
> With gifts and graces eminently adorned,
> To some great work, thy glory
>     And people's safety, *which in part they effect.*"

And here, I must venture a remark on the ambiguity of the expressions concerning our author's Montanism. In the treatise against Marcion, written late in his career, Tertullian identifies himself with the Church and strenuously defends its faith and its apostolic order. In only rare instances does his weakness for the "new prophecy" crop out, and then, it is only as one identifies himself with a school within the church. Precisely so Fenelon maintained his milder Montanism, without a thought of deserting the Latin Church. Afterwards Fenelon drew back, but at last poor Tertullian fell away. So with the Jansenists. They credited the *miracles* and the *convulsions* (or ecstasies) of their school, and condemned those who rejected them, as Tertullian condemns the *Psychics*. The great expounder of the Nicene Faith (Bp. Bull) does indeed speak very decidedly of Tertullian as a *lapser*, even when he wrote his first book against Marcion. His semi-schismatic position must be allowed. But, was it a *formal* lapse at that time? The English non-jurors were long in communion with the Church, even while they denounced their brethren and the "Erastianizing" clergy, much as Tertullian does the *Psychics*. St. Augustine speaks of *Tertullianists* with great moderation, and notes the final downfall of our author as something distinct from Tertullianism. When we reflect, therefore, that only four of all his varied writings (now extant) are proofs of an accomplished lapse, ought we not carefully to maintain the distinction between the Montanistic Tertullian and Tertullian the Montanist? Bishop Bull, it seems to me would not object to this way of putting it, when we consider his own discrimination in the following weighty words. He says:

"A clear distinction must be made between those works which Tertullian, when already a Montanist, wrote specifically in defense of Montanism *against the church*, and those which he composed, as a Montanist indeed, yet *not in defense of Montanism against the church*, but rather, *in defense of the common doctrines of the church*—and of Montanus, in opposition to other heretics."

Now in arranging the works of this second class, *the Prescription* comes logically first, because, written in Orthodoxy, it forcibly upholds the Scriptural Rule of Faith, the Catholic touchstone of all professed verity. It is also a necessary Introduction to the great work against Marcion which I have placed next in order; giving it the precedence to which it is entitled in part on chronological ground, in part because of the general purity of its material with the exhibition it presents of the author's mental processes and of his very gradual decline from Truth.

Very fortunate were the Edinburgh Editors in securing for this work and some others, the valuable labors of Dr. Holmes, of whom I have elsewhere given some biographical particulars. The merit and fullness of his annotations are so marked, that I have been spared a great deal of work, such as I was forced to bestow on the former volumes of this American Edition. But on the other hand these pages have given me much patient study and toil as an editor, because of the "shreds and patches" in which Tertullian comes to us, in the Edinburgh Series; and because of some typographical peculiarities, exceptional in that Series itself, and presenting complications, when transferred to a new form of mechanical arrangement.

For example, apart from some valuable material which belongs to the General Preface, and which I have transferred accordingly, the following dislocations confronted me to begin with: The *Marcion* is presented to us in Volume VII. apart from the other writings of Tertullian. At the close of Vol. XI. we reach the *Ad Nationes*, of which Dr. Holmes is the translator, another hand (Mr. Thelwall's) having been employed on former pages of that volume. It is not till we reach Volume XV. that Tertullian again appears, but this volume is wholly the work of Dr. Holmes. Finally, in Volume XVIII., we meet Tertullian again, (Mr. Thelwall the able translator), but, here is placed the "Introduction" to all the works of

Tertullian, which, of course, I have, transferred to its proper place. I make these explanations by no means censoriously, but to point out at once the nature of my own task, and the advantage that accrues to the reader, by the order in which the works of the great Tertullian appear in this edition, enabling him to compare different or parallel passages, all methodically arranged in consecutive pages, without a minute's search, or delay.

Now, as to typographical difficulties to which I have referred, Dr. Holmes marks all his multiplied and useful notes with *brackets*, which are almost always superfluous, and which in this American Edition are used to designate my own contributions, when printed with the text, or apart from Preface and Elucidations. These, therefore, I have removed necessarily and with no appreciable loss to the work, but great gain to the beauty of the page. But, again, Dr. Holmes' translations are all so heavily bracketed as to become an eyesore, and the disfigured pages have been often complained of as afflictive to the reader. Many words strictly implied by the original Latin, and which should therefore be unmarked, are yet put between brackets. Even minute words (*and*, or *to wit*, or *again*,) when, in the nature of the case the English idiom requires them, are thus marked. I have not retained these blemishes; but when an inconsiderable word or a repetition does add to the sense, or qualify it, I have italicized such words, throwing more important interpolations into parenthetical marks, which are less painful to the sight than brackets. I have found them quite as serviceable to denote the auxiliary word or phrase; and where the author himself uses a parenthesis, I have observed very few instances in which a sensible reader would confound it with the translator's efforts to eke out the sense. Sometimes, an awkward interpolation has been thrown into a footnote.

Occasionally the crabbed sentences of the great Carthaginian are so obscure that Dr. Holmes has been unable to make them lucid, although, with the original in hand, he probably felt a force in his own rendering which the mere English reader must fail to perceive. In a few such instances, noting the fact in the margin, I have tried to bring out the sense, by slight modifications of punctuation and arrangement. Occasionally too I have dropped a superfluous interpolation (such as *e.g., to conclude*, or let me say again,) when I have found that it only served to clog and overcharge a sentence. Last of all, Dr. Holmes' *headings* have sometimes been condensed, to avoid phrases and sentences immediately recurring in the chapter. These purely mechanical parts require a terse form of statement, like those in the English Bible, and I have frequently reduced them on that model, dropping redundant adverbs and adjectives to bring out the catchwords.

Ad Martyras and The Passion of the Holy Martyrs Perpetua and Felicitas

# Ad Martyras.

Chapter I.

Blessed Martyrs Designate, —Along with the provision which our lady mother the Church from her bountiful breasts, and each brother out of his private means, makes for your bodily wants in the prison, accept also from me some contribution to your spiritual sustenance; for it is not good that the flesh be feasted and the spirit starve: nay, if that which is weak be carefully looked to, it is but right that that which is still weaker should not be neglected. Not that I am specially entitled to exhort you; yet not only the trainers and overseers, but even the unskilled, nay, all who choose, without the slightest need for it, are wont to animate from afar by their cries the most accomplished gladiators, and from the mere throng of onlooker's useful suggestions have sometimes come; first, then, O blessed, grieve not the Holy Spirit, who has entered the prison with you; for if He had not gone with you there, you would not have been there this day. Do you give all endeavor, therefore, to retain Him; so let Him lead you thence to your Lord. The prison, indeed, is the devil's house as well, wherein he keeps his family. But you have come within its walls for the very purpose of trampling the wicked one under foot in his chosen abode. You had already in pitched battle outside utterly overcome him; let him have no reason, then, to say to himself, "They are now in my domain; with vile hatreds I shall tempt them, with defections or dissensions among themselves." Let him fly from your presence, and skulk away into his own abysses, shrunken and torpid, as though he were an out charmed or smoked-out snake. Give him not the success in his own kingdom of setting you at variance with each other, but let him find you armed and fortified with concord; for peace among you is battle with him. Some, not able to find this peace in the Church, have been used to seek it from the imprisoned martyrs. And so you ought to have it dwelling with you, and to cherish it, and to guard it, that you may be able perhaps to bestow it upon others.

Chapter II.

Other things, hindrances equally of the soul, may have accompanied you as far as the prison gate, to which also your relatives may have attended you. There and thenceforth you were severed from the world; how much more from the ordinary course of worldly life and all its affairs! Nor let this separation from the world alarm you; for if we reflect that the world is more really the prison, we shall see that you have gone out of a prison rather than into one. The world has the greater darkness, blinding men's hearts. The world imposes the more grievous fetters, binding men's very souls. The world breathes out the worst impurities—human lusts. The world contains the larger number of criminals, even the whole human race. Then, last of all, it awaits the judgment, not of the proconsul, but of God. Wherefore, O blessed, you may regard yourselves as having been translated from a prison to, we may say, a place of safety. It is full of darkness, but ye yourselves are light; it has bonds, but God has made you free. Unpleasant exhalations are there, but ye are an odor of sweetness. The judge is daily looked for, but ye shall judge the judges themselves. Sadness may be there for him who sighs for the world's enjoyments. The Christian outside the prison has renounced the world, but in the prison he has renounced a prison too. It is of no consequence where you are in the world—you who are not of it. And if you have lost some of life's sweets, it is the way of business to suffer present loss, that after gains may be the larger. Thus far I say nothing of the rewards to which God invites the martyrs. Meanwhile let us compare the life of the world and of the prison, and see if the spirit does not gain more in the prison than the flesh loses. Nay, by the care of the Church and the love of the brethren, even the flesh does not lose there what is for its good, while the spirit obtains besides important advantages. You have no occasion to look on strange gods, you do not run against their images; you have no part in heathen holidays, even by mere bodily mingling in them; you are not annoyed by the foul fumes of idolatrous solemnities; you are not pained by the noise of the public shows, nor by the atrocity or madness or immodesty of their celebrants; your eyes do not fall on stews and brothels; you are free from causes of offence, from temptations, from unholy reminiscences; you are free now from persecution too. The prison does the same service for the Christian which the desert did for the prophet. Our Lord Himself spent much of His time in seclusion, that He might have greater liberty to pray, that He might be quit of the world. It was in a mountain solitude, too, He showed His glory to the disciples. Let us drop the name of prison; let us call it a place of retirement. Though the body is shut in, though the flesh is confined, all things are open to the spirit. In spirit, then, roam abroad; in spirit walk about, not setting before you shady paths or long colonnades, but the way which leads to God. As often as in spirit your footsteps are there, so often you will not be in bonds. The leg does not feel the chain when the mind is in the heavens. The mind compasses the whole man about, and whither it wills it carries him. But where thy heart shall be, there shall be thy treasure. Be there our heart, then, where we would have our treasure.

Chapter III.

Grant now, O blessed, that even to Christians the prison is unpleasant; yet we were called to the warfare of the living God in our very response to the sacramental words. Well, no soldier comes out to the campaign laden with luxuries, nor does he go to action from his comfortable chamber, but from the light and narrow tent, where every kind of hardness, roughness and unpleasantness must be put up with. Even in peace soldiers inure themselves to war by toils and inconveniences—marching in arms, running over the plain, working at the ditch, making the testudo, engaging in many arduous labors. The sweat of the brow is on everything, that bodies and minds may not shrink at having to pass from shade to sunshine, from sunshine to icy cold, from the robe of peace to the coat of mail, from silence to clamor, from quiet to tumult. In like manner, O blessed ones, count whatever is hard in this lot of yours as a discipline of your powers of mind and body. You are about to pass through a noble struggle, in which the living God acts the part of superintendent, in which the Holy Ghost is your trainer, in which the prize is an eternal crown of angelic essence, citizenship in the heavens, glory everlasting. Therefore, your Master, Jesus Christ, who has anointed you with His Spirit, and led you forth to the arena, has seen it good, before the day of conflict, to take you from a condition more pleasant in itself, and has imposed on you a harder treatment, that your strength might be the greater. For the athletes, too, are set apart to a more stringent discipline, that they may have their physical powers built up. They are kept from luxury, from daintier meats, from more pleasant drinks; they are pressed, racked, worn out; the harder their labors in the preparatory training, the stronger is the hope of victory. "And they," says the apostle, "that they may obtain a corruptible crown." We, with the crown eternal in our eye, look upon the prison as our training-ground, that at the goal of final judgment we may be brought forth well disciplined by many a trial; since virtue is built up by hardships, as by voluptuous indulgence it is overthrown.

Chapter IV.

From the saying of our Lord we know that the flesh is weak, the spirit willing. Let us not, withal, take delusive comfort from the Lord's acknowledgment of the weakness of the flesh. For precisely on this account He first declared the spirit willing, that He might show which of the two ought to be subject to the other—that the flesh might yield obedience to the spirit—the weaker to the stronger; the former thus from the latter getting strength. Let the spirit hold convene with the flesh about the common salvation, thinking no longer of the troubles of the prison, but of the wrestle and conflict for which they are the preparation. The flesh, perhaps, will dread the merciless sword, and the lofty cross, and the rage of the wild beasts, and that punishment of the flames, of all most terrible, and all the skill of the executioner in torture. But, on the other side, let the spirit set clearly before both itself and the flesh, how these things, though exceeding painful, have yet been calmly endured by many, —and, have even been eagerly desired for the sake of fame and glory; and this not only in the case of men, but of women too, that you, O holy women, may be worthy of your sex. It would take me too long to enumerate one by one the men who at their own self-impulse have put an end to themselves. As to women, there is a famous case at hand: the violated Lucretia, in the presence of her kinsfolk, plunged the knife into herself, that she might have glory for her chastity. Mucius burned his right hand on an altar, that this deed of his might dwell in fame. The philosophers have been outstripped, —for instance Heraclitus, who, smeared with cow dung, burned himself; and Empedocles, who leapt down into the fires of Ætna; and Peregrinus, who not long ago threw himself on the funeral pile. For women even have despised the flames. Dido did so, lest, after the death of a husband very dear to her, she should be compelled to marry again; and so did the wife of Hasdrubal, who, Carthage being on fire, that she might not behold her husband suppliant as Scipio's feet, rushed with her children into the conflagration, in which her native city was destroyed. Regulus, a Roman general, who had been taken prisoner by the Carthaginians, declined to be exchanged for a large number of Carthaginian captives, choosing rather to be given back to the enemy. He was crammed into a sort of chest; and, everywhere pierced by nails driven from the outside, he endured so many crucifixions. Woman has voluntarily sought the wild beasts, and even asps, those serpents worse than bear or bull, which Cleopatra applied to herself, that she might not fall into the hands of her enemy. But the fear of death is not so great as the fear of torture. And so the Athenian courtesan succumbed to the executioner, when, subjected to torture by the tyrant for having taken part in a conspiracy, still making no betrayal of her confederates, she at last bit off her tongue and spat it in the tyrant's face, that he might be convinced of the uselessness of his torments, however long they should be continued. Everybody knows what to this day is the great Lacedæmonian solemnity—the διαμαστύγωσις, or scourging; in which sacred rite the Spartan youths are beaten with scourges before the altar, their parents and kinsmen standing by and exhorting them to stand it bravely out. For it will be always counted more honorable and glorious that the soul rather than the body has given itself to stripes. But if so high a value is put on the earthly glory, won by mental and bodily vigor, that men, for the praise of their fellows, I may say, despise the sword, the fire, the cross, the wild beasts, the torture; these surely are but trifling sufferings to obtain a celestial glory and a divine reward. If the bit of glass is so precious, what must the true pearl be worth? Are we not called on, then, most joyfully to lay out as much for the true as others do for the false?

Chapter V.

I leave out of account now the motive of glory. All these same cruel and painful conflicts, a mere vanity you find among men—in fact, a sort of mental disease—as trampled underfoot. How many ease-lovers does the conceit of arms give to the sword? They actually go down to meet the very wild beasts in vain ambition; and they fancy themselves more winsome from the bites and scars of the contest. Some have sold themselves to fires, to run a certain distance in a burning tunic. Others, with most enduring shoulders, have walked about under the hunters' whips. The Lord has given these things a place in the world, O blessed, not without some reason: for what reason, but now to animate us, and on that day to confound us if we have feared to suffer for the truth, that we might be saved, what others out of vanity have eagerly sought for to their ruin?

Chapter VI.

Passing, too, from examples of enduring constancy having such an origin as this, let us turn to a simple contemplation of man's estate in its ordinary conditions, that mayhap from things which happen to us whether we will or no, and which we must set our minds to bear, we may get instruction. How often, then, have fires consumed the living! How often have wild beasts torn men in pieces, it may be in their own forests, or it may be in the heart of cities, when they have chanced to escape from their dens! How many have fallen by the robber's sword! How many have suffered at the hands of enemies the death of the cross, after having been tortured first, yes, and treated with every sort of contumely! One may even suffer in the cause of a man what he hesitates to suffer in the cause of God. In reference to this indeed, let the present time bear testimony, when so many persons of rank have met with death in a mere human being's cause, and that though from their birth and dignities and bodily condition and age such a fate seemed most unlikely; either suffering at his hands if they have taken part against him, or from his enemies if they have been his partisans.

# Introductory Notice to the Martyrdom of Perpetua and Felicitas.

Nobody, will blame me for placing here the touching history of these Martyrs. It illustrates the period of history we are now considering, and sheds light on the preceding treatise. I can hardly read it without tears, and it ought to make us love "the noble army of martyrs." I think Tertullian was the editor of the story, not its author. Felicitas is mentioned by name in the De Anima: and the closing paragraph of this memoir is quite in his style. To these words I need only add that Dr. Routh, who unfortunately decided not to re-edit it, ascribes the first edition to Lucas Holstenius. He was Librarian of the Vatican and died in 1661. The rest may be learned from this Introductory Notice of the Translator:

Perpetua and Felicitas suffered martyrdom in the reign of Septimius Severus, about the year 202 a.d.Tertullian mentions Perpetua, and a further clue to the date is given in the allusion to the birth-day of "Geta the Cæsar," the son of Septimius Severus. There is therefore, good reason for rejecting the opinion held by some, that they suffered under Valerian and Gallienus. Some think that they suffered at Tuburbium in Mauritania; but the more general opinion is, that Carthage was the scene of their martyrdom.

The "Acta," detailing the sufferings of Perpetua and Felicitas, has been held by all critics to be a genuine document of antiquity. But much difference exists as to who was the compiler. In the writing itself, Perpetua and Saturus are mentioned as having written certain portions of it; and there is no reason to doubt the statement. Who the writer of the remaining portion was, is not known. Some have assigned the work to Tertullian; some have maintained that, whoever the writer was, he was a Montanist, and some have tried to show that both martyrs and narrator were Montanists. The narrator must have been a contemporary; according to many critics, he was an eye-witness of the sufferings of the martyrs. And he must have written the narrative shortly after the events.

Dean Milman says, "There appear strong indications that the acts of these African martyrs are translated from the Greek; at least it is difficult otherwise to account for the frequent untranslated Greek words and idioms in the text.

The Passion of Perpetua and Felicitas was edited by Petrus Possinus, Rome, 1663; by Henr. Valesius, Paris, 1664; and the Bollandists. The best and latest edition is by Ruissart, whose text is adopted in Gallandi's and Migne's collections of the Fathers.

# The Passion of the Holy Martyrs Perpetua and Felicitas.

Preface.

If ancient illustrations of faith which both testify to God's grace and tend to man's edification are collected in writing, so that by the perusal of them, as if by the reproduction of the facts, as well God may be honored, as man may be strengthened; why should not new instances be also collected, that shall be equally suitable for both purposes,—if only on the ground that these modern examples will one day become ancient and available for posterity, although in their present time they are esteemed of less authority, by reason of the presumed veneration for antiquity? But let men look to it, if they judge the power of the Holy Spirit to be one, according to the times and seasons; since some things of later date must be esteemed of more account as being nearer to the very last times, in accordance with the exuberance of grace manifested to the final periods determined for the world. For "in the last days, saith the Lord, I will pour out of my Spirit upon all flesh; and their sons and their daughters shall prophesy. And upon my servants and my handmaidens will I pour out of my Spirit; and your young men shall see visions, and your old men shall dream dreams." And thus we—who both acknowledge and reverence, even as we do the prophecies, modern visions as equally promised to us, and consider the other powers of the Holy Spirit as an agency of the Church for which also He was sent, administering all gifts in all, even as the Lord distributed to every one as well needfully collect them in writing, as commemorate them in reading to God's glory; that so no weakness or despondency of faith may suppose that the divine grace abode only among the ancients, whether in respect of the condescension that raised up martyrs, or that gave revelations; since God always carries into effect what He has promised, for a testimony to unbelievers, to believers for a benefit. And we therefore, what we have heard and handled, declare also to you, brethren and little children, that as well you who were concerned in these matters may be reminded of them again to the glory of the Lord, as that you who know them by report may have communion with the blessed martyrs, and through them with the Lord Jesus Christ, to whom be glory and honor, for ever and ever. Amen.

Chapter I.—Argument. —When the Saints Were Apprehended, St. Perpetua Successfully Resisted Her Father's Pleading, Was Baptized with the Others, Was Thrust into a Filthy Dungeon. Anxious About Her Infant, by a Vision Granted to Her, She Understood that Her Martyrdom Would Take Place Very Shortly.

1. The young catechumens, Revocatus and his fellow-servant Felicitas, Saturninus and Secundulus, were apprehended. And among them also was Vivia Perpetua, respectably born, liberally educated, a married matron, having a father and mother and two brothers, one of whom, like herself, was a catechumen, and a son an infant at the breast. She herself was about twenty-two years of age. From this point onward she shall herself narrate the whole course of her

martyrdom, as she left it described by her own hand and with her own mind.

2. "While" says she, "we were still with the persecutors, and my father, for the sake of his affection for me, was persisting in seeking to turn me away, and to cast me down from the faith, — 'Father,' said I, 'do you see, let us say, this vessel lying here to be a little pitcher, or something else?' And he said, 'I see it to be so.' And I replied to him, 'Can it be called by any other name than what it is?' And he said, 'No.' 'Neither can I call myself anything else than what I am, a Christian.' Then my father, provoked at this saying, threw himself upon me, as if he would tear my eyes out. But he only distressed me, and went away overcome by the devil's arguments. Then, in a few days after I had been without my father, I gave thanks to the Lord; and his absence became a source of consolation to me. In that same interval of a few days we were baptized, and to me the Spirit prescribed that in the water of baptism nothing else was to be sought for bodily endurance. After a few days we are taken into the dungeon, and I was very much afraid, because I had never felt such darkness. O terrible day! O the fierce heat of the shock of the soldiery, because of the crowds! I was very unusually distressed by my anxiety for my infant. There were present there Tertius and Pomponius, the blessed deacons who ministered to us, and had arranged by means of a gratuity that we might be refreshed by being sent out for a few hours into a pleasanter part of the prison. Then going out of the dungeon, all attended to their own wants. I suckled my child, which was now enfeebled with hunger. In my anxiety for it, I addressed my mother and comforted my brother, and commended to their care my son. I was languishing because I had seen them languishing on my account. Such solicitude I suffered for many days, and I obtained for my infant to remain in the dungeon with me; and forthwith I grew strong and was relieved from distress and anxiety about my infant; and the dungeon became to me as it

were a palace, so that I preferred being there to being elsewhere.

3. "Then my brother said to me, 'My dear sister, you are already in a position of great dignity, and are such that you may ask for a vision, and that it may be made known to you whether this is to result in a passion or an escape.' And I, who knew that I was privileged to converse with the Lord, whose kindnesses I had found to be so great, boldly promised him, and said, 'To-morrow I will tell you.' And I asked, and this was what was shown me. I saw a golden ladder of marvelous height, reaching up even to heaven, and very narrow, so that persons could only ascend it one by one; and on the sides of the ladder was fixed every kind of iron weapon. There were there swords, lances, hooks, daggers; so that if any one went up carelessly, or not looking upwards, he would be torn to pieces and his flesh would cleave to the iron weapons. And under the ladder itself was crouching a dragon of wonderful size, who lay in wait for those who ascended, and frightened them from the ascent. And Saturus went up first, who had subsequently delivered himself up freely on our account, not having been present at the time that we were taken prisoners. And he attained the top of the ladder, and turned towards me, and said to me, 'Perpetua, I am waiting for you; but be careful that the dragon does not bite you.' And I said, 'In the name of the Lord Jesus Christ, he shall not hurt me.' And from under the ladder itself, as if in fear of me, he slowly lifted up his head; and as I trod upon the first step, I trod upon his head. And I went up, and I saw an immense extent of garden, and in the midst of the garden a white-haired man sitting in the dress of a shepherd, of a large stature, milking sheep; and standing around were many thousand white-robed ones. And he raised his head, and looked upon me, and said to me, 'Thou art welcome, daughter.' And he called me, and from the cheese as he was milking he gave me as it were a little cake, and I received it with folded hands; and I ate it, and all who stood around said Amen. And at the sound of their voices I was awakened, still tasting a sweetness

which I cannot describe. And I immediately related this to my brother, and we understood that it was to be a passion, and we ceased henceforth to have any hope in this world.

Chapter II. —Argument. Perpetua, When Besieged by Her Father, Comforts Him. When Led with Others to the Tribunal, She Avows Herself a Christian, and is Condemned with the Rest to the Wild Beasts. She Prays for Her Brother Dinocrates, Who Was Dead.

1. "After a few days there prevailed a report that we should be heard. And then my father came to me from the city, worn out with anxiety. He came up to me, that he might cast me down, saying, 'Have pity my daughter, on my grey hairs. Have pity on your father, if I am worthy to be called a father by you. If with these hands I have brought you up to this flower of your age, if I have preferred you to all your brothers, do not deliver me up to the scorn of men. Have regard to your brothers, have regard to your mother and your aunt, have regard to your son, who will not be able to live after you. Lay aside your courage, and do not bring us all to destruction; for none of us will speak in freedom if you should suffer anything.' These things said my father in his affection, kissing my hands, and throwing himself at my feet; and with tears he called me not Daughter, but Lady. And I grieved over the grey hairs of my father, that he alone of all my family would not rejoice over my passion. And I comforted him, saying, 'On that scaffold whatever God wills shall happen. For know that we are not placed in our own power, but in that of God.' And he departed from me in sorrow.

2. "Another day, while we were at dinner, we were suddenly taken away to be heard, and we arrived at the town-hall. At once the rumor spread through the neighborhood of the public place, and an immense number of people were gathered together. We mount the platform. The rest were interrogated, and confessed. Then they came to me, and my father

immediately appeared with my boy, and withdrew me from the step, and said in a supplicating tone, 'Have pity on your babe.' And Hilarianus the procurator, who had just received the power of life and death in the place of the proconsul Minucius Timinianus, who was deceased, said, 'Spare the grey hairs of your father, spare the infancy of your boy, offer sacrifice for the well-being of the emperors.' And I replied, 'I will not do so.' Hilarianus said, 'Are you a Christian?' And I replied, 'I am a Christian.' And as my father stood there to cast me down from the faith, he was ordered by Hilarianus to be thrown down, and was beaten with rods. And my father's misfortune grieved me as if I myself had been beaten, I so grieved for his wretched old age. The procurator then delivers judgment on all of us, and condemns us to the wild beasts, and we went down cheerfully to the dungeon. Then, because my child had been used to receive suck from me, and to stay with me in the prison, I send Pomponius the deacon to my father to ask for the infant, but my father would not give it him. And even as God willed it, the child no long desired the breast, nor did my breast cause me uneasiness, lest I should be tormented by care for my babe and by the pain of my breasts at once.

3. "After a few days, whilst we were all praying, on a sudden, in the middle of our prayer, there came to me a word, and I named Dinocrates; and I was amazed that that name had never come into my mind until then, and I was grieved as I remembered his misfortune. And I felt myself immediately to be worthy, and to be called on to ask on his behalf. And for him I began earnestly to make supplication, and to cry with groaning to the Lord. Without delay, on that very night, this was shown to me in a vision. I saw Dinocrates going out from a gloomy place, where also there were several others, and he was parched and very thirsty, with a filthy countenance and pallid color, and the wound on his face which he had when he died. This Dinocrates had been my brother after the flesh, seven years of age who died miserably with disease—his face being so eaten out with cancer, that his death caused repugnance to

all men. For him I had made my prayer, and between him and me there was a large interval, so that neither of us could approach to the other. And moreover, in the same place where Dinocrates was, there was a pool full of water, having its brink higher than was the stature of the boy; and Dinocrates raised himself up as if to drink. And I was grieved that, although that pool held water, still, on account of the height to its brink, he could not drink. And I was aroused, and knew that my brother was in suffering. But I trusted that my prayer would bring help to his suffering; and I prayed for him every day until we passed over into the prison of the camp, for we were to fight in the camp-show. Then was the birth-day of Geta Cæsar, and I made my prayer for my brother day and night, groaning and weeping that he might be granted to me.

4. "Then, on the day on which we remained in fetters, this was shown to me. I saw that that place which I had formerly observed to be in gloom was now bright; and Dinocrates, with a clean body well clad, was finding refreshment. And where there had been a wound, I saw a scar; and that pool which I had before seen, I saw now with its margin lowered even to the boy's navel. And one drew water from the pool incessantly, and upon its brink was a goblet filled with water; and Dinocrates drew near and began to drink from it, and the goblet did not fail. And when he was satisfied, he went away from the water to play joyously, after the manner of children, and I awoke. Then I understood that he was translated from the place of punishment.

Chapter III. —Argument. Perpetua is Again Tempted by Her Father. Her Third Vision, Wherein She is Led Away to Struggle Against an Egyptian. She Fights, Conquers, and Receives the Reward.

1. "Again, after a few days, Pudens, a soldier, an assistant overseer of the prison, who began to regard us in great esteem, perceiving that the great power of God was in us,

admitted many brethren to see us, that both we and they might be mutually refreshed. And when the day of the exhibition drew near, my father, worn with suffering, came in to me, and began to tear out his beard, and to throw himself on the earth, and to cast himself down on his face, and to reproach his years, and to utter such words as might move all creation. I grieved for his unhappy old age.

2. "The day before that on which we were to fight, I saw in a vision that Pomponius the deacon came hither to the gate of the prison, and knocked vehemently. I went out to him, and opened the gate for him; and he was clothed in a richly ornamented white robe, and he had on manifold calliculæ. And he said to me, 'Perpetua, we are waiting for you; come!' And he held his hand to me, and we began to go through rough and winding places. Scarcely at length had we arrived breathless at the amphitheater, when he led me into the middle of the arena, and said to me, 'Do not fear, I am here with you, and I am laboring with you;' and he departed. And I gazed upon an immense assembly in astonishment. And because I knew that I was given to the wild beasts, I marveled that the wild beasts were not let loose upon me. Then there came forth against me a certain Egyptian, horrible in appearance, with his backers, to fight with me. And there came to me, as my helpers and encouragers, handsome youths; and I was stripped, and became a man. Then my helpers began to rub me with oil, as is the custom for contest; and I beheld that Egyptian on the other hand rolling in the dust. And a certain man came forth, of wondrous height, so that he even overtopped the top of the amphitheater; and he wore a loose tunic and a purple robe between two bands over the middle of the breast; and he had on calliculæ of varied form, made of gold and silver; and he carried a rod, as if he were a trainer of gladiators, and a green branch upon which were apples of gold. And he called for silence, and said, 'This Egyptian, if he should overcome this woman, shall kill her with the sword; and if she shall conquer him, she shall receive this branch.' Then he departed. And we

drew near to one another, and began to deal out blows. He sought to lay hold of my feet, while I struck at his face with my heels; and I was lifted up in the air, and began thus to thrust at him as if spurning the earth. But when I saw that there was some delay I joined my hands so as to twine my fingers with one another; and I took hold upon his head, and he fell on his face, and I trod upon his head. And the people began to shout, and my backers to exult. And I drew near to the trainer and took the branch; and he kissed me, and said to me, 'Daughter, peace be with you:' and I began to go gloriously to the Sanavivarian gate. Then I awoke, and perceived that I was not to fight with beasts, but against the devil. Still I knew that the victory was awaiting me. This, so far, I have completed several days before the exhibition; but what passed at the exhibition itself let who will write."

Chapter IV. —Argument. Saturus, in a Vision, and Perpetua Being Carried by Angels into the Great Light, Behold the Martyrs. Being Brought to the Throne of God, are Received with a Kiss. They Reconcile Optatus the Bishop and Aspasius the Presbyter.

1. Moreover, also, the blessed Saturus related this his vision, which he himself committed to writing: — "We had suffered," says he, "and we were gone forth from the flesh, and we were beginning to be borne by four angels into the east; and their hands touched us not. And we floated not supine, looking upwards, but as if ascending a gentle slope. And being set free, we at length saw the first boundless light; and I said, 'Perpetua' (for she was at my side), 'this is what the Lord promised to us; we have received the promise.' And while we are borne by those same four angels, there appears to us a vast space which was like a pleasure-garden, having rose-trees and every kind of flower. And the height of the trees was after the measure of a cypress, and their leaves were falling incessantly. Moreover, there in the pleasure-garden four other angels appeared,

brighter than the previous ones, who, when they saw us, gave us honor, and said to the rest of the angels, 'Here they are! Here they are!' with admiration. And those four angels who bore us, being greatly afraid, put us down; and we passed over on foot the space of a furlong in a broad path. There we found Jocundus and Saturninus and Artaxius, who having suffered the same persecution were burnt alive; and Quintus, who also himself a martyr had departed in the prison. And we asked of them where the rest were. And the angels said to us, 'Come first, enter and greet your Lord.'

2. "And we came near to place, the walls of which were such as if they were built of light; and before the gate of that place stood four angels, who clothed those who entered with white robes. And being clothed, we entered and saw the boundless light, and heard the united voice of some who said without ceasing, 'Holy! Holy! Holy!' And in the midst of that place we saw as it were a hoary man sitting, having snow-white hair, and with a youthful countenance; and his feet we saw not. And on his right hand and on his left were four-and-twenty elders, and behind them a great many others were standing. We entered with great wonder, and stood before the throne; and the four angels raised us up, and we kissed Him, and He passed His hand over our face. And the rest of the elders said to us, 'Let us stand;' and we stood and made peace. And the elders said to us, 'Go and enjoy.' And I said, 'Perpetua, you have what you wish.' And she said to me, 'Thanks be to God, that joyous as I was in the flesh, I am now more joyous here.'

3. "And we went forth, and saw before the entrance Optatus the bishop at the right hand, and Aspasius the presbyter, a teacher, at the left hand, separate and sad; and they cast themselves at our feet, and said to us, 'Restore peace between us, because you have gone forth and have left us thus.' And we said to them, 'Art not thou our father, and thou our presbyter, that you should cast yourselves at our feet?' And we prostrated ourselves, and we embraced them; and Perpetua began to speak with them, and we drew them apart in the

pleasure-garden under a rose-tree. And while we were speaking with them, the angels said unto them, 'Let them alone, that they may refresh themselves; and if you have any dissensions between you, forgive one another.' And they drove them away. And they said to Optatus, 'Rebuke thy people, because they assemble to you as if returning from the circus, and contending about factious matters.' And then it seemed to us as if they would shut the doors. And in that place we began to recognize many brethren, and moreover martyrs. We were all nourished with an indescribable odor, which satisfied us. Then, I joyously awoke."

Chapter V.—Argument. Secundulus Dies in the Prison. Felicitas is Pregnant, but with Many Prayers She Brings Forth in the Eighth Month Without Suffering, the Courage of Perpetua and of Saturus Unbroken.

1. The above were the more eminent visions of the blessed martyrs Saturus and Perpetua themselves, which they themselves committed to writing. But God called Secundulus, while he has yet in the prison, by an earlier exit from the world, not without favor, so as to give a respite to the beasts. Nevertheless, even if his soul did not acknowledge cause for thankfulness, assuredly his flesh did.

2. But respecting Felicitas (for to her also the Lord's favor approached in the same way), when she had already gone eight months with child (for she had been pregnant when she was apprehended), as the day of the exhibition was drawing near, she was in great grief lest on account of her pregnancy she should be delayed, —because pregnant women are not allowed to be publicly punished, —and lest she should shed her sacred and guiltless blood among some who had been wicked subsequently. Moreover, also, her fellow-martyrs were painfully saddened lest they should leave so excellent a friend, and as it were companion, alone in the path of the same hope. Therefore, joining together their united cry, they poured forth

their prayer to the Lord three days before the exhibition. Immediately after their prayer her pains came upon her, and when, with the difficulty natural to an eight months' delivery, in the labor of bringing forth she was sorrowing, some one of the servants of the Cataractarii said to her, "You who are in such suffering now, what will you do when you are thrown to the beasts, which you despised when you refused to sacrifice?" And she replied, "Now it is I that suffer what I suffer; but then there will be another in me, who will suffer for me, because I also am about to suffer for Him." Thus she brought forth a little girl, which a certain sister brought up as her daughter.

3. Since then the Holy Spirit permitted, and by permitting willed, that the proceedings of that exhibition should be committed to writing, although we are unworthy to complete the description of so great a glory; yet we obey as it were the command of the most blessed Perpetua, nay her sacred trust, and add one more testimony concerning her constancy and her loftiness of mind. While they were treated with more severity by the tribune, because, from the intimations of certain deceitful men, he feared lest they should be withdrawn from the prison by some sort of magic incantations, Perpetua answered to his face, and said, "Why do you not at least permit us to be refreshed, being as we are objectionable to the most noble Cæsar, and having to fight on his birth-day? Or is it not your glory if we are brought forward fatter on that occasion?" The tribune shuddered and blushed, and commanded that they should be kept with more humanity, so that permission was given to their brethren and others to go in and be refreshed with them; even the keeper of the prison trusting them now himself.

4. Moreover, on the day before, when in that last meal, which they call the free meal, they were partaking as far as they could, not of a free supper, but of an agape; with the same firmness they were uttering such words as these to the people, denouncing against them the judgment of the Lord, bearing witness to the felicity of their passion, laughing at the curiosity

of the people who came together; while Saturus said, "To-morrow is not enough for you, for you to behold with pleasure that which you hate. Friends today, enemies to-morrow. Yet note our faces diligently, that you may recognize them on that day of judgment." Thus all departed thence astonished, and from these things many believed.

Chapter VI. —Argument. From the Prison They are Led Forth with Joy into the Amphitheatre, Especially Perpetua and Felicitas. All Refuse to Put on Profane Garments. They are Scourged, They are Thrown to the Wild Beasts. Saturus Twice is Unhurt. Perpetua and Felicitas are Thrown Down; They are Called Back to the Sanavivarian Gate. Saturus Wounded by a Leopard, Exhorts the Soldier. They Kiss One Another, and are Slain with the Sword.

1. The day of their victory shone forth, and they proceeded from the prison into the amphitheater, as if to an assembly, joyous and of brilliant countenances; if perchance shrinking, it was with joy, and not with fear. Perpetua followed with placid look, and with step and gait as a matron of Christ, beloved of God; casting down the luster of her eyes from the gaze of all. Moreover, Felicitas, rejoicing that she had safely brought forth, so that she might fight with the wild beasts; from the blood and from the midwife to the gladiator, to wash after childbirth with a second baptism. And when they were brought to the gate, and were constrained to put on the clothing—the men, that of the priests of Saturn, and the women, that of those who were consecrated to Ceres—that noble-minded woman resisted even to the end with constancy. For she said, "We have come thus far of our own accord, for this reason, that our liberty might not be restrained. For this reason, we have yielded our minds, that we might not do any such thing as this: we have agreed on this with you." Injustice acknowledged the justice; the tribune yielded to their being brought as simply as they were. Perpetua sang psalms, already treading underfoot

the head of the Egyptian; Revocatus, and Saturninus, and Saturus uttered threatenings against the gazing people about this martyrdom. When they came within sight of Hilarianus, by gesture and nod, they began to say to Hilarianus, "Thou judgest us," say they, "but God will judge thee." At this the people, exasperated, demanded that they should be tormented with scourges as they passed along the rank of the venatores. And they indeed rejoiced that they should have incurred any one of their Lord's passions.

2. But He who had said, "Ask, and ye shall receive," gave to them when they asked, that death which each one had wished for. For when at any time they had been discoursing among themselves about their wish in respect of their martyrdom, Saturninus indeed had professed that he wished that he might be thrown to all the beasts; doubtless that he might wear a more glorious crown. Therefore, in the beginning of the exhibition he and Revocatus made trial of the leopard, and moreover upon the scaffold they were harassed by the bear. Saturus, however, held nothing in greater abomination than a bear; but he imagined that he would be put an end to with one bite of a leopard. Therefore, when a wild boar was supplied, it was the huntsman rather who had supplied that boar who was gored by that same beast, and died the day after the shows. Saturus only was drawn out; and when he had been bound on the floor near to a bear, the bear would not come forth from his den. And so Saturus for the second time is recalled unhurt.

3. Moreover, for the young women the devil prepared a very fierce cow, provided especially for that purpose contrary to custom, rivalling their sex also in that of the beasts. And so, stripped and clothed with nets, they were led forth. The populace shuddered as they saw one young woman of delicate frame, and another with breasts still dropping from her recent childbirth. So, being recalled, they are unbound. Perpetua is first led in. She was tossed, and fell on her loins; and when she saw her tunic torn from her side, she drew it over her as a veil for her middle, rather mindful of her modesty than her

suffering. Then she was called for again, and bound up her disheveled hair; for it was not becoming for a martyr to suffer with disheveled hair, lest she should appear to be mourning in her glory. So she rose up; and when she saw Felicitas crushed, she approached and gave her her hand, and lifted her up. And both of them stood together; and the brutality of the populace being appeased, they were recalled to the Sanavivarian gate. Then Perpetua was received by a certain one who was still a catechumen, Rusticus by name, who kept close to her; and she, as if aroused from sleep, so deeply had she been in the Spirit and in an ecstasy, began to look around her, and to say to the amazement of all, "I cannot tell when we are to be led out to that cow." And when she had heard what had already happened, she did not believe it until she had perceived certain signs of injury in her body and in her dress, and had recognized the catechumen. Afterwards causing that catechumen and the brother to approach, she addressed them, saying, "Stand fast in the faith, and love one another, all of you, and be not offended at my sufferings."

4. The same Saturus at the other entrance exhorted the soldier Pudens, saying, "Assuredly here I am, as I have promised and foretold, for up to this moment I have felt no beast. And now believe with your whole heart. Lo, I am going forth to that beast, and I shall be destroyed with one bite of the leopard." And immediately at the conclusion of the exhibition he was thrown to the leopard; and with one bite of his he was bathed with such a quantity of blood, that the people shouted out to him as he was returning, the testimony of his second baptism, "Saved and washed, saved and washed." Manifestly he was assuredly saved who had been glorified in such a spectacle. Then to the soldier Pudens he said, "Farewell, and be mindful of my faith; and let not these things disturb, but confirm you." And at the same time he asked for a little ring from his finger, and returned it to him bathed in his wound, leaving to him an inherited token and the memory of his blood. And then lifeless he is cast down with the rest, to be

slaughtered in the usual place. And when the populace called for them into the midst, that as the sword penetrated into their body they might make their eyes partners in the murder, they rose up of their own accord, and transferred themselves whither the people wished; but they first kissed one another, that they might consummate their martyrdom with the kiss of peace. The rest indeed, immoveable and in silence, received the sword-thrust; much more Saturus, who also had first ascended the ladder, and first gave up his spirit, for he also was waiting for Perpetua. But Perpetua, that she might taste some pain, being pierced between the ribs, cried out loudly, and she herself placed the wavering right hand of the youthful gladiator to her throat. Possibly such a woman could not have been slain unless she herself had willed it, because she was feared by the impure spirit.

O most brave and blessed martyrs! O truly called and chosen unto the glory of our Lord Jesus Christ! whom whoever magnifies, and honors, and adores, assuredly ought to read these examples for the edification of the Church, not less than the ancient ones, so that new virtues also may testify that one and the same Holy Spirit is always operating even until now, and God the Father Omnipotent, and His Son Jesus Christ our Lord, whose is the glory and infinite power for ever and ever. Amen.

Elucidations.

(Dinocrates, cap. ii. p. 701.)

The avidity with which the Latin controversial writers seize upon this fanciful passage, (which, in fact, is subversive of their whole doctrine about Purgatory, as is the text from the Maccabees) makes emphatic the utter absence from the early Fathers of any reference to such a dogma; which, had it existed, must have appeared in every reference to the State of the Dead, and in every account of the discipline of penitents. Arbp.

Usher ingeniously turns the tables upon these errorists, by quoting the Prayers for the Dead, which were used in the Early Church, but which, such as they were, not only make no mention of a Purgatory, but refute the dogma, by their uniform limitation of such prayers to the blessed dead, and to their consummation of bliss at the Last day and not before. Such a prayer seems to occur in 2 Tim. i. 18. The context (vers. 16–18, and iv. 19) strongly supports this view; Onesiphorus is spoken of as if deceased, apparently. But, as Chrysostom understands it, he was only absent (in Rome) from his household. From i. 17we should infer that he had left Rome.

Printed by Libri Plureos GmbH in Hamburg, Germany